Ecoepic

& other poems

Ken Ingham

Ecoepic
& other poems

ISBN 978-1-84728-959-9

This book was published through lulu.com
Additional copies are available on line at
www.lulu.com/ingham

Contents

Ecoepic

& Other Poems

"The ideal writing life would be one spent endlessly embroidering one enormous poem."
poet Scott Cairns

Ecoepic
Part I.

Evolution
of Tumorous Times

In the beginning
13 ± 2 billion years ago
Before creation
Before the start of any race
There was a nothingness, a void
A vacuum full of time
And curvature of empty space
Mass was negative
And traveled faster
Than the speed of light
If there was any
And numbers were only imaginary

Then, on *Day One*

The boredom of the gods imploded
Black and heavy holes exploded
Antimatter converted to matter
Big bangs of fire, hot gasses
Birth pangs of milky ways
Drifting orbiting molten masses

One of which Earth
Just happened to settle
The optimum distance from its star
Not like Mercury hot and close
Or Pluto cold and far

Spinning precisely once each day
Albeit with a bit of a wobble
Circadian by definition
And most improbable
For unknown reasons
Its axis tilted toward the ecliptic
Enough to effect perennial seasons

Earth's vapors cooled
Dark clouds drooled
Moon and rain provided rhythm
Primordial soups bestirred by tides
The hope of life abided within them

Simple elements in the first three rows
Ionized and radicalized by radiation
Formed increasingly complex structures
Heteroatomic combinations

Carboxyl and amino groups
Stereospecific methylenes
Phosphorylribosyl purines and pyrimidines
Diffusing colliding condensing contriving
The ternary secrets of self-replication

Four-letter alphabet, three-letter words
Arranged in future conditional tense
Sentences, paragraphs, whole declarations
Interspersed with apparent nonsense

Random instructions for peptide assembly
Combinatorial in the extreme
Twenty options at each position
With infinite time to screen

To pick and choose from enormous pools
Of N-mers as if by intelligent design
Selecting the ones that were stable and able
To fold and survive in the brine

Backbones twisted, a helix flickered
Hydrophobic side chains collapsed in a core
Between two beta pleated sheets
Eventually enzymes were born

Bearing unique shapes and surface grooves
That fostered specific interactions
And catalyzed what would otherwise
Be very slow reactions

Amphipathic lipids coalesced
Into semipermeable microspheres
Trapping proteins and nucleic acids
This went on for a billion years
Then near the end of the *Second Day*
(don't ask me how -- it's hard to say)
A tiny germ of life appeared

That dubious progenitor
Divided multiplied swam and crawled
Differentiated, discovered sex
Oooooohoohoohooh!
Simple organisms evolved

In which each cell suppressed its self
Its ego subsumed by that of the whole
A cooperative community
One body one soul

One mind one will
Seeking its fill
Defying the laws of entropy
Filtering sifting mutating drifting
Lifting up out of the sea.

And that was *Day Three*

Gradually improbably
Through a dozen periods of geology
There stretched over Earth
An elastic stocking, a resilient web
Of interdependent living forms
Connected by threads of ecology

And all of this from a single cell?
Yes according to Alberts *et al.*
In the leading bible of biology

Air was clear, water pure
Lush green plants with fruit to share
Furry animals reptiles birds
Diverse species everywhere

Their tracks adorned muddy paths
Like those I trod in childhood
Songs and howls, croaks and growls
Echoed through the neighborhood

And on *Day Four*
The gods thought all was good

Plants and animals, yin and yang
Exchanging oxygen for CO_2
Each individual a link in the chain
An integral part of a larger milieu

Whole biomes slithered up and down
The longitudes at less than snail speed
Breathing in phase with the changing albedo
As glaciers advanced and receded

Herbivorous brontosauri
Feasted freely on the green
Fossils don't tell us how or why
They vanished from the scene

Perhaps they ate too many trees
Maybe a virus brought them down
More likely a comet from outer space
Collided with the ground

Raising a cloud of opaque dust
Extinguishing the status quo
Making *Day Five* a difficult time
For anything to grow

Meanwhile
Eons of sunlight had been converted
To photosynthetic fossil fuels
Huge reserves of free energy
Hidden away like family jewels
In the basements of antiquity
Deep in subterranean pools
Waiting for a gifted species
To discover and learn to use

At last on *Day Six*
Came forth *Homo sapiens*
Endowed with much advantage
With clever thumbs we beat our drums
Elaborated thoughts and language
Gestures sounds verbs and nouns
To represent ten thousand things
Primitive pictures, burial mounds
Symbols of life after death with wings

We built fires in our caves
To stay warm and up late
To intimidate our predators
And cook the meat we ate

To celebrate
In the flickering night
We danced and chanted
Took nothing for granted
The gods were glad to have made us
Intuitively we worshiped the Sun
The One God that has never betrayed us

Look! there it is again !

Rising in silence over the meer
We cupped our ears to imagine the sound
Of a nurturing fire too far to hear
Yet hot enough to turn skin brown

We joined together for the hunt
Domesticated fowl and cattle
Cultivated grain and fruit
Gave the horse a saddle
A stirrup a halter a harness a bit
A wagon a plow a buggy to pull
We tanned hides combed cotton
Wove wool

We subdued most of our natural foes
Dominated land and sea
Then up against each other rose
Fighting for freedom and democracy

With public schools and powerful tools
Life improved without limit
Hunting and fishing became mere sports
The new world's bounty seemed infinite

Estuaries ripe with crunchy crustaceans
Nine foot sturgeon with bushels of roe
Skies overflown with *bonnie plump* pigeons
Great plains embroidered with sweet buffalo
In endless columns
They roamed through tall grasses
Pulverizing thick grub-rich loam
Whole towns of black-tailed prairie dogs
Stood vigilant near their burrowed homes
While sixty million beaver
Maintained the riparian zones

All this was ours for the taking
For food for fun for decoration
But there wasn't enough
For Cro-Magnons with guns
To share with indigenous
Fourth World Nations

We specialized, industrialized
All resources were assailed
Men in white coats hypothesized
Science and technology prevailed

Antibiotics insecticides
Internal combustion engines
Subatomic electricity
Wireless communication

We were so smart we understood all
But that about which we dared not think:
The nature of that mysterious force
That draws our species toward the brink

That causes us to overconsume
To pollute and overpopulate
To saturate our living room
With chemicals designed to exterminate
Weeds and pests and anything inedible
That germinates against our will
Or competes with a crop
Endocrine disrupters that percolate
Through a tadpole's gill
And rise to the top of the chain
To come to rest in a woman's breast
Or concentrate in someone's brain

= = = = = =

Rachel was the first to bring
Attention to the tanks unloading
The (dis)content of her *Silent Spring*
Was frank and foreboding

Cactus Ed Abbey ruthlessly wrenched
His monkey message to the fore
The human spirit hung in the balance
According to Albert Gore

Wendell Berry wrote at home
While rotating crops on a *Gift of Good Land*
Carefully chosen words that bemoan
The passing of doing things by hand

Many people perceived the danger
And tried their best to publicize
Yet institutions were slow to change
Collectively we seemed paralyzed

Unable to agree or compromise
On what our goal should be
Unwilling to acknowledge
Our addiction to free energy

Frequent flyers filled the air
Combining business with pleasure
Ignoring or pretending to be unaware
Or just didn't care
About the finite nature of our treasure

Asphalt highways, no fault insurance
Two cars for every couple
Gasoline was cheaper than bottled water
And about as much trouble

Filling stations on every corner
Slip your plastic into the slot
Five minutes later back on the road
Walking became obsolete

Virgin forests almost depleted
Lumber was needed for second homes
Wrap-around decks, pressure-treated
With cupric arsenate and hexavalent chrome

Wood chip yards with gazebos in the middle
Particle board manufactured afloat
Railroad ties and telephone poles
That dribble toxic creosote

Into the streams now become storm sewers
Chlorine-bleached paper mills
Disposable chopsticks, shish kabob skewers
Pallets diapers napkins towels
Café Americano cups in huge piles
Company prospectuses and annual reports
Grant proposals and legal files
Extra long paper mandated by courts

= = = = = =

So many species seeking survival
Competing for food and space
But few were blessed
With enough finesse
To compete with the human race

Six billion strong on a logarithmic roll
Global average three babies per girl
Net ten thousand new people each hour
Yes,
     we were the champions
      we were the champions
       we were the champions
      of the world

Higher still higher the standards grew
Our appetites grew quicker
Sky and water no longer blue
The biosphere was getting sicker

Three Mile Island, Rocky Flats
That little town in Missouri
Love Canal, Bhopal
Be Happy, Don't Worry

That pain in your chest
That lump on your breast
Is it malignant or benign?
CANCER – the name of a tropic
Or an astrological sign

Under which
A single cell becomes confused
By a molecule not previously seen
An impostor a synthetic ruse
That slithers into the space between
Opposing faces of DNA bases
Causing a frame shift point mutation
De-repressing the ego gene
Triggering unchecked replication

One makes two makes four makes eight
Ad nauseam ad infinitum
Add chemo then irradiate
Try to shrink the growth inside
Imperious doctors rolling eyes
Mumbling about lymph and bone marrow
My best friend is about to die; outside
The sound of an angel's voice disguised
As that of a sweet song sparrow

And he just one of thousands each year
Who succumb to that hideous disease
We need clean water, we need clean air
We need to get up off our knees
And resist the technoindustrial goliath
Forever on the verge of a cure
Insist that prevention get more attention
Endeavor to keep our environment pure

= = = = = =

Oh how I yearn for humorous rhymes
Or that Jesus would descend from heaven
With a miracle for these tumorous times
Dear God wake up! It's been too long *Day Seven*

Ecoepic
Part II.

Disciples of Gaia

One thousand Points of Light he said
An aptly ambiguous metaphor
Evoking distant campfires at night
Or glow worms on the forest floor

One thousand Points of Light he repeated
Pointing and waving his arm like a wand.
Who me? said those
Whose angst had been seeded
By *Civil Disobedience* and *Walden Pond.*

They felt a sense of guilt and shame
Knew that something must be done
Would only have themselves to blame . . .
But the good life kept them on the run

With busy jobs and families
Their time was all consumed
Not much left for politics
Yet up ahead disaster loomed

They saw this, it hit them
whenever they paused
Long enough to absorb some alternative news

While go-stopping to and from shopping or work
Car radios tuned to a station with blues

A collusion of interests, not in their own
Or that of their loved ones was gaining momentum
Becoming more powerful than their government
Which increasingly failed to represent them

They joined good clubs and paid their dues
Lobbied Congress for their cause
Letters were written, phone calls made
But they changed too slow, the laws

And the laws already on the books
Were rarely if ever dispensed
Fines were trivial compared to profits
Another deductible business expense

Enron, World Com, Adelphia, Quest
Merrill Lynch, Global Crossing and Tyco
Arthur Anderson, all the rest
Far too many to list in a Haiku

Exxon Valdez, Chico Mendez
What ever happened to justice?
All the leaders ever said was
read my lips
trust us
read my lips
trust us ....

Life was too short
Points of Light couldn't wait
Their precious children faced the dark
Something had to give, one day
As if two twigs had lit a spark
As if 't were in the good book written
Eco enemy number one
Mysteriously was smitten

While driving alone through Rock Creek Park
In his mistress's convertible turbo Ferrari
Stuck in the neck by a well-blown dart
Loaded with deadly d-tubocurare

Yes someone finally felt that strong
Why should anyone have been surprised?
Assassination for far too long
Had been limited to troublesome good guys

Those for whose help the wilderness yearns
An anonymous internet message read
Quietly take your respective turns
Until all the scoundrels are dead

No signature, no credits claimed
It must have been some psycho nut
But Points of Light could not ignore
The odd sensation in their gut

How could they feel so warm inside
Over anyone's execution?
Gradually they realized
They were in the midst of a revolution

Yet killing to them was not an option
To kill was to yield the moral advantage
Selective destruction of property
Was less risky and easier to manage

Without interrupting their careers
Without even knowing each other
Silently they volunteered
To act on behalf of their common Mother

Most were moved to lesser crimes
Becoming creative and skilled practitioners
Sabotaging motor homes
Central air conditioners
Cabin cruisers, snowmobiles
Ride-on mowers, ATCs
They drained oil from caterpillars
Painted furs, spiked trees

A few played for higher stakes
Detonating bridges and dams
Overturning tractor trailers
Triggering rush hour traffic jams
Toppling cell towers, hacking computers
Creatively misusing superglue
Torching the (empty) houses and
Headquarters of the you know who

Who?

The list of the names
Of those affected
Confirmed the main idea
The targets were the plunderers
Who terrorize Gaia
CEO's in fancy clothes
From the dozen dirtiest corporations
Rare species dealers, habitat stealers
Corrupt deceitful politicians
Turtle smashers, baby seal bashers
Toxic dumpers and pesticide pumpers
Blatantly dishonest greenwashers, brownlashers
Heartless greedy old growth stumpers . . . .

= = = = = =

The powers that be were panicky
Suspicious staff were fired
Urine was tested, e-mail collected
Guards with dogs were hired
Barbed wire fences brick walls trenches
Security gates where all must stop
To be inspected or else get ejected
By private Humvees with turrets on top

The big three-letter agencies
Scanned gigabytes of classified files
Pointing and clicking relentlessly seeking
Someone to bring to trial

Scratching their heads, chewing their nails
They struggled for a clue
An inkling of conspiracy
But none came into view

The plot to rescue Mother Earth
Would never be detected
In fact there wasn't one
Just random disconnected acts
By people nobody suspected

Gaia be damned!
The meek were struck
Each cheek in turn was bruised.
The plunderers could stand no more
Their orders being refused

With phony warrants
They searched the homes
Of radical ecodefense leaders

Analyzed the chromosomes
Of Earth First! Journal readers

The offices of Green Peace
Sea Shepard and Sierra Club
Were placed under covert surveillance
ALF and ELF, long at the hub
Were infiltrated by secret agents

You're either for us or against us
The president said
Blind to shades of green and gray
Ecoterrorism will not stand
A smart bomb hit Tucson that day

People were jailed and not apprized
Trumped up charges brought to bear
And those who dared to sympathize
Were watched with utmost care

But this was not USSR
Libertarians soon bristled
ACLU knew what to do
Insiders loudly whistled

Hearings were broadcast in minute detail
Trials by digital high definition
But most Points of Light eluded jail
As juries were hung by indecision

At odds over what was right or wrong
Unwilling to swallow establishment pabulum
Some brave jurors had minds of their own
And refused to sit back and play dumb

Not since slavery or Viet Nam
Had the line so clearly been drawn
There was no room to vacillate
Which side would you have been on?

Ecoepic
Part III.

Dawning
of the Eighth Day

For several years the battle raged,
Some scenes were too gross to mention
But extremism always helps
To focus the people's attention
Those who used to turn their heads
In spite of all the proof
Were sensitized by Points of Light
And wanted now to know the truth

They opened up their sticky eyes
Their hearts and minds became like sponges
Groundswell quests for truth were launched
In hillbilly bars and yuppie lounges
In coffee houses all over the world
On the internet, in the workplace
Deep conversations of great substance
About the goal, the purpose, the mission, if any
Of the highly intelligent human race

Rationality was important
No opinion could be blind
Assertions made with no support
Were challenged or left behind
Books that previously went unread
Became dog-eared and tattered

Thoughts once muttered or left unsaid
Were now uttered as if they mattered

Arguments broke out, composures cracked
But most their tempers controlled
An obscure poet/playwright strove to extract
The highlights of the story that was being told

Imagine a stage where actors enter
All assuming different stances
Then taking turns front and center
To deliver the following stanzas

= = = = = = =

Go to hell
You tree huggin' son of a bitch!
Who asked for your stupid opinion?
Don't tell me I can't dig a ditch
On the land over which
I've been given dominion
I bought this swamp decades ago
Useless mud, mosquito infested
Now drained and filled, it's ready to go
For many returns on what was invested

Invested by whom
You greedy capitalist developer schnook
Your contribution is minuscule
Compared to the thousands of years that it took
To establish this oozing vestibule
Where runoff pauses to give up pollutants
Before entering the Chesapeake Bay
Where amphibians thrive, ducks dabble and dive
Small mammals and raptors breed and play
Then along comes one thoughtless wimp
With a bulldozer
To destroy it in a single day

Look Buddy
People want new homes near the water
Where they can watch the osprey catch fish
Who are you to stand in the way
Of me fulfilling their wish?
It's a free country
It's a matter of supply and demand
It's an opportunity to get ahead
They have the money, I have the land

This land belongs not just to you
Other species live here too
Wild animals need space to roam
It's wrong to keep them in a zoo
As it was wrong to relegate
Red people to reservations
More so now to annihilate
The Big Blue Heron's habitation

Marbled Murrelet! Spotted Owl
What's all the freekin' fuss?
I don't want to lose my job
If its them or us, I vote for us
I've got payments to make, mouths to feed
Why should I forsake a profit?

This is my property – look, here's my deed
Now why don't you just get off it!

Listen!
Property rights are a human construct
Animals don't recognize our boundaries
Deer leap fences, bears cross state lines
Birds traverse latitudes of many degrees
This Earth is theirs and ours to share
We're all becoming endangered creatures
Each animal and plant, each organism
Has unique and worthy features

Damn right! Including me!
Don't forget
God created heaven and earth
And all that grows beneath the skies
And then made man and unto man
Bequeathed these things to utilize

No way!
Nature was never ours to own
Just a loan to ease our mourn
Left by the dead for we the living
Borrowed from the yet unborn

(whose numbers grow in spite of all
the efforts to forewarn)

                                    Hey!
                  It's written in the Bible, Nerd
                         Be fruitful and multiply
                  Who are you to question the word
                  Of the Lord Almighty God on High?
                     Start a family! Conceive! Beget!
                  Spread your progeny yon and hither
                     Fill the land with believers and let
                         The lowly heathens wither

But for what end? Whose will be done
If all the Earth is blemished?
In that same breath that same god said
That Earth should be *replenished*
i.e., once again made full and complete
That's the meaning of God's plan
Remember, God also created

Wilderness
wherein there be
no roads or man

43

Saying further:

Hurt not the earth
nor the sea nor the trees
defile it not with detestable things
speak to the earth and it shall teach thee
Ye have no preeminence over a beast.

Oh come on –
Human beings don't blemish the earth
Are you a misanthrope of some kind?
If you're so down on civilization
How do you hope to change its mind?

Civilization?
I remember when that word meant
The opposite of barbarism
Literature art music science
The hard-won fruits of martyrism
But viewed by Indian braves and squaws
Or from the standpoint of ancient trees
Civilization becomes the main cause
Of Gaia's spreading skin disease

I concede
Modern living takes a toll
But your prose exaggerates the cons
Tell me which do you prefer
Master bathrooms or outdoor johns?
Paris, London, New York, Rome
These weren't built with magic wands
Great cities of the world my friend
Are not the work of leprechauns

If great cities symbolize collective achievement
The edge of the wedge of what is humane
Then we should all be in affective bereavement
Our cities are writhing in pain
Their inflammation festers outward
Grays replacing greens and blues
Obliterating open space
Expanding the size of the bruise

But you must admit
You love down town, the parks and squares
The underground Metro stations
Ethnic restaurants, theaters, shoppes
Political demonstrations
Second hand book stores, libraries

Courses at the university . . . .
The many faces of different races
The cultural diversity

Diversity ? Don't be preposterous!
Let's not confuse the meaning of words
The number of species in a given metropolis
Varies inversely with the tonnage of turds
Dropped, flushed, processed and mixed
With parking lot runoff, dumped in the river
Suffocating fish and macro-invertebrates
Poisoning someone down stream's liver

And those who dwell in the highest towers
With the most elaborate plumbing
Can't wait to escape with their purchasing power
The islanders applaud their coming
Send us your rich and weary masses
Desperately seeking peace of mind
We've got plenty of lower classes
To cheaply provide what you leave behind
With scuba gear and four wheel drives
They encroach upon real diversity
Hotels appear, development thrives
Soon there's just another city

46

I can't believe your attitude
Don't be so easily fooled
Would you prefer an older world
Where lions and tigers ruled
Where danger lurked
Behind each bush
Snakes d
      a
        n
          g
          l
         e
          d
From every tree
And hungry hyenas
Cast silhouettes tall
On the moonlit wall
Of your flimsy tipi
Or maybe an even earlier time
When fire was a mystery
That sometimes happened
After a storm
When winter was more
Than a time to get warm
By the stove
Reading history

No!
We don't want to go back in time
Say women more often than men
In spite of all the drugs and crime
Life is better than it was then

Before the machines and appliances
That ease our drudgery
Before the advent of law and order
The judge and jury
Before the end of robber barons
Before the slaves were set afloat
Before women inched out from under men
And clinched their right to vote

But also my Dear
Before weapons of mass destruction
Before the word fire became a verb
Before the fascists made it illegal
To partake of the seven-leafed herb

And before we learned in such detail
The ecosystems of our planet
Before Earth as we knew it became so frail
Before humanity over-ran it

Here is the truth that makes me shudder
Honey, if not even we can agree
How can we hope to convert the others
In time to avert a catastrophe?

You see,
Many of our problems ultimately stem
From the inequality of the sexes
But heaven forbid if women ever did
To men what they could with their hexes
Men like to think they're in control
But women since the time of the nomads
Have quietly practiced the marital art
Of manipulating men through their gonads

It's true!
Testosterone is potent stuff
It regulates the macho genes
Induces rutting butting and strutting
Especially in the middle teens
When horns are grown and oats are sewn
And boys do what ever they fuckin' wanna
The remedy is simple enough
Just legalize marijuana

Oh Please! Don't be absurd
I can't believe you're serious
Giving boys marijuana?
You must be delirious

Not at all
Tetrahydrocannabinol
Though still inadequately tested
Is clearly safer than alcohol
Aside from the risk of getting arrested

Making marijuana illegal is smart
That drug impairs memory and motivation
Distorts time, accelerates the heart
Induces paranoia and hallucinations

Hey, you didn't mention cancer and lung disease
And what about expectant mothers?
Let's face it, all drugs can be abused
But some are worse than others
Tobacco kills half a million each year
Booze destroys whole communities
Yet cigarettes snuff liquor and beer
Are advertised and sold with impunity

Marijuana is just the first step
A gateway to harder stuff
Starting out with a toke may seem hep
Soon they'll be rolling up their cuff

The fact is,
Legalization of that innocent plant
Could diminish the market for harder drugs
By allowing folks to get what they want
Without doing business with criminal thugs
Who lace the leaf with stronger stuff
Hoping to get you hooked and craving
To the point where you are desperate enough
To give them your entire life's savings

But tokers act and look so dopey
With their dilated pupils and bloodshot eyes
Their fascination with flickering lights
Their inexplicable giggles . . .

What about their aversion to picking fights?
Is that so despicable?

Fancy a program to introduce the weed
Responsibly, of course, at appropriate times

51

As a right of passage when taking the creed
With lighting of candles and ringing of chimes

Thereafter used in modest amounts
An occasional pinch in the morning with cereal
Could lower global testosterone counts
Engendering peace and good will

Yeah sure, what then?
Feminism? Love in the street?
Sexual preferences freely disclosed?
No more reason to be discreet
Let's all smile and take off our clothes
Get in a pile and do to each other
Whatever each other
Would want the other to do

Ah, but human beings are so abundant
And soaring eagles so precious few
And far between
When occasionally seen
Close up through my field glasses
I sense that my love for vanishing birds
Exceeds my love for the human masses

Consider this:
When it comes to social
evolution our species has yet
to fully flower. While sometimes
sharing and helping each other, more
often we fight over money and power
over food and land, oil and water, or
to settle a historical score. For
reasons we don't understand
we're caught in a vortex
of violence
and war.
We
need
to practice
resolving conflicts
making collective decisions.
We need to formulate common goals,
articulate collective visions, to identify
issues on which we concur, write them
into our constitution. It takes a majority
of at least two thirds but its less traumatic
than revolution. Those issues on which
nobody agrees should be debated
over fences, across all social
boundaries, an ongoing
search for global
consensus.

Right on brother!
But what about the animals?
Who will speak on their behalf?
The wolf, the whale, the salmon the quail
The pigs and the cows - don't laugh!
Much of the land we cultivate
To feed the animals we eat
Could be restored to a natural state
If we could get by with less meat

        Beans and rice, tofu and spice, that's
        What little vegans are made of, I wonder
           How do they manage to stay alive
        They look like they're dying of hunger

(Actually, they'll probably live longer)

You know
Vegetarianism might have seemed stupid
In a jungle full of beasts that would eat us
But now the jungle is null and void
The world is dripping with humanoids
Who break out in fights
While debating the rights
Of another ill-conceived unwanted fetus

Sad!
Millions of mammals from monkeys to mice
Bred to die on laboratory benches
Organs swapped, genes excised
Where draw the lines?
Where dig the trenches?

How else are we to learn the ABC's
Of mammalian physiology
In sufficient detail to cure disease
Or advance the field of xenobiology?

Speaking of which

I need to fix my broken heart
It can't sustain me too much longer
I need a quick cardiac jumpstart
Please call the local organ-monger
Find me a ticker that won't get rejected
A baboon's or gorilla's wouldn't be bad
But I'll pay quicker and more than expected
For one from a healthy lass or lad

Question:
Is it fair to take the throbbing heart
Of a vanishing distant cousin
To spare the life of a rich old fart
When humans are a dime a dozen?

I think not said Ishmael
Through the bars of his circus wagon
With haunting eyes that mesmerize
He asked me: try to imagine
That you were vanishing and we were in charge
How would you like to live in a cage
Waiting around for your next injection
Of hepatitis or AIDS?
What makes you think you're so special
So different from me and the chimpanzee?
What if your creation story is wrong?
What if God views us all equally?
What then will happen if after you die
And arriving at heaven's security gate
The guard on duty checking credentials
Turns out to be a hairy primate?

If you had paid more
attention in bible school
You would know that's highly improbable
And as for AIDS
That's just God's way
Of punishing the abominable
Those promiscuous swappers of bodily fluids
Most of whom were offered The Answer
But refused to repent and continued to do it
Even when faced with the prospect of cancer

Who knows The Answer, no one for sure
We're the first species to even care
The first to ask about the hereafter
Maybe the first to become aware
Enough to evolve a global conscience
The Noösphere of Vernadsky
and de Chardin
An epigenetic memetic ethic
Empirically rooted in the land

One thing for sure
We are unique, the way we think
Our capacity for empathy and sorrow
What other species is able to link
Yesterday with now and tomorrow?
We visualize, extrapolate
Comprehend portentous trends
We realize if only of late
It is us upon whom the future depends
This awareness presses down
Demands that we explore
The essence of our inner selves
Try to put an end to war
Not just war between each other
But war against our fellow critters
The kingdoms of plants and animals
For whom we've become the sitters
And thinkers and wonderers
The ones with a vision of what could be
If those who advocate peace, save the whales
Could only get through to the rest of thee
(Especially you wannabe alpha males)

You're too romantic! Impractical!
The threat of war will always be
A strong defense is critical
To save us from the enemy

Who feigns belief in world freedom
Then flouts international law
Too much clout in those hands
Could bring to a boil what once was a thaw
An era of arrogance shock and awe
A superpower that admits no flaw
Arrests its own without due cause
Exempts its military from environmental laws

Racism
Fascism
Terrorism
Nationalism
Ethnic Cleansing
Religious Fundamentalism
Innocent victims caught in the crunch
And underlying all of these, the most
insidious of the bunch
Speciesism

Wilderness whispers its urgent request
In the trees, soft music, can you hear it?
Imploring us to cease and desist
And give gist to the human spirit
That sense of hope, that confidence
That common desire for common good
That growing body of knowledge
That vision, if only we could .   .   .

Lots o' luck!
The vision thing
Seems to have disappeared
The values of the now/me generation
Were commandeered by marketeers
Of instant gratification
As if each day might be their last
They grew up with a vision of horror
Like Henny Pennys waiting for
The sky to fill with nuclear war

Yes . . . . . still

Say it softly

Nuclear war

And what about their progeny
Born before *The Day After* aired?
Caution - this program contains material
That will make your children really scared!

End of History, End of Nature
End of Oil and the American Dream
Who can afford a detached home
Let alone a cabin by a stream?

Whoa! Cheer up!
There's no reason to be so blue
We've got supply side economics
And market forces to pull us through

Yes, market forces, read my lips
Will solve the current conundrum
Wealth will fall upon the rich
And trickle down to all those under 'em

Hurumph!
Trickle down, yeah, sure, how crass
Your choice of metaphor is strange
What trickles down to the working class
Are the pebbles and crumbs, the small change

Market forces, like wild horses, stampede
On their own without provocation
Free range capitalism unimpeded
Will drive the Earth into privation

                    No it won't
                 Not if we get a reign
           On those over-reaching bureaucrats
            They're the problem if you ask me
            Get the regulators off our backs
               Antitrust is blasphemy
                Cut the capital gains tax
        Insure Silverado Savings and Loan
           Military: prepare for attacks
            On multiple sides of the globe

    Woe is me
Even if we all agreed
How can we change the way we live
When the Bottom Line requires that
We take more than we give?

            Oh Bottom Line, in thee we trust
             Thou symbol of financial health
          Now black now red, now boom now bust
          Sweet measure of success and wealth

The Bottom Line has come to be
An object of deification
Worthy of human sacrifice
On the altar of corporate salvation

Oh Bottom Line I pledge to thee
To never paint thee red
When e'er the ink is turning pink
I'll simply roll another head
A theme to spread around the world
West, from Milan to Venice
Give me profit, or give me death!
Annihilate the Great Red menace

Give me the Bottom Line, dammit!
Just give me the Bottom Line!

I can't!
The magnitude and sign of the Bottom Line
Depend on how computed
Depletion deductions are asinine
How could we have been so deluded?
The precious oil that goes to waste
Millions of barrels of crude are spilled

And natural gas consumed in haste
So we can get nude in the winter, unchilled

                              OK! I get the point!
                    Eliminate waste! Abolish greed!
                          But let the fossil fuel flow
                       Cheap energy is guaranteed
                       To make our economy grow

Growth? Growth!
I'm sick of growth!
Our growth economy sucks!
Our Mother's Milk relentlessly
And shits it out the other end
Of mostly empty pickup trucks
And vans and sedans as fast as it can
With no alternative in sight
But when our Mother's breast runs dry . . .
Day will be day . . . . .
And night shall once again be night

Petroleum is about to peak
And natural gas soon after in turn
At the rate its being consumed today
My grandkids will see the last of it burn

And then what?

No problem,
We'll bake the oil out of Wyoming's shale
(And devastate the Green River Basin?)
Distill ethanol from biomass ale
(Feed cars instead of starving nations?)
We'll strip mine the tar sands of Athabasca
(Obliterate Alberta's bogs and fens?)
And eventually drill all over Alaska
(No way - Points of Light will reignite before then)

And of course
There will always be nukes
Quiet, clean, no soot no smoke
No harmful greenhouse gases
No acid rain, and when they're broke
Just tuck them into Gaia's crevasses

Yeah but . . . .
What institution could ever outstay
The multi-millennial half-lives
To oversee the natural decay
Of those hot and heavy nuclei?

Deadly plutonium leaches still
From Chernobyl's cracked sarcophagi
The spines of Grenoble sustain a chill
At the thought of a similar tragedy

Not to worry!
The engineers have now perfected
A foolproof failsafe fission reactor
The probability of major release
Has been reduced to a trivial factor

Huh!
Trivial say those with great compose
Whose livelihoods belie their bias
Smiling at us down their nose
Their arguments don't satisfy us
They can't guarantee an accident free
Nuke no matter how wired
Foolproof indeed they'd better be
Who else but a fool would agree to be hired?

They're all fools, forgive them Lord
They know not what they do
And if I choose to smite a few
It's not because I don't love you

Its just that, well
There's too many people
And not enough food to feed them all
And the Pope says to hell with birth control
Except for premature withdrawal
(or abstinence for those who respond
to the highest call)

Get hold of yourself, your too up tight
There's no reason to panic yet
According to the latest polls
The doomsday sayers are soakin' wet
There's food enough to feed the world
Even the hordes in the barrios
Thomas Malthus was a wimp
I'm sick of these dire scenarios!

Polls don't measure truth, Boy Scout
The masses are largely uninformed
Most can't even think about
The reasons why the earth has warmed
They watch insipid TV shows
Sponsored by free enterprise
And if they get their shopping done
They'll vote for the best advertized

I swear!
To hear you going off like that
I wonder if you went to school
You do believe in democracy, don't you?
You do believe in majority rule?

Of course I believe in democracy
Ain't never been nothin' better
I learned that before I earned
my high school varsity letter
Constitution, Bill of Rights
The evils of commun ~~ity~~ ism,
Adam Smith, Henry Ford
The marvels of capitalism

But the forefathers didn't anticipate
One of democracy's little imperfections
The extent to which those who incorporate
Would come to influence public elections
With checkbooks ready they circle the obelisk
Smug in their corporate personhood
With all of its benefits and none of the risk
A thug doesn't worry about the common good
If you truly believe in democracy
Then you'll love this antidote:

Let's put the charters of the Fortune 500
To a periodic popular vote

yeeGads!
Take him away!

How would we compete with other nations
In the game now played on global stages
Which if we win will give us the jobs
With the easiest work and the highest wages
NAFTA and GATT are where it's at
The rules on which the coaches agree

But . . .
The players are quick to notice that
There ain't enough referees
The season seems to never end
The box office never closes
And keeping score is such a chore
When you don't even know what the goal is

With all due respect, can you tell me
What we are trying so hard to build?
When we've completed our various missions
What conditions will be fulfilled?
Will there be peace and prosperity?
How many weeks off with pay?

Will everyone have a second home
In the mountains overlooking the Bay?
A car for work, a car for play
A closet full of three piece suits?
Will we be allowed to loiter in the meadow
Making love and playing flutes?

Get serious you socialist yippee!
You probably voted for LBJ.
That Great Society of welfare Hippies
Unwilling to pay their own way.
Gimmee gimmee gimmee gimmee!
That stuff drives me berserk.
If you pay people for being lazy
Why would anybody work?

Here's why! Listen up!
A peer's approval, a neighbor's respect
A pat on the back when in need
These are true sources of motivation
Alternatives to money and greed
Inner peace, meaningful work
Progress toward a worthy cause
Affirmation, a friendly hug
Gentle teasing, a few guffaws, Yes!

Uncontrolled laughter, tears of joy
These are what we're working for
They cleanse the heart, revive the soul
And pump us up to work some more

                    Oh brother!
              You are off the deep end
              Materialism is here to stay
          After millions of years of evolution
               It's locked up in our DNA
(Like being straight or being gay?)
                    It's all been prearranged
              Like getting old and turning gray
              Let's accept what we can't change
          Here, have another glass of Dubonet

          Drink to Darwin, survival of the fittest

Drink by yourself you deranged fatalist!
I'm not in the mood to down one now
I want to stimulate change, be a catalyst
Turn the trends around somehow
I believe in human potential
To recognize and mend collective errors

I want to help make things better
For yours and my children and theirs
(& theirs & theirs & theirs . . . . . .)
Its gonna happen, in our lifetime
Were getting smarter every day
If you don't want to participate
Please . . .
Get thee but out of the way!

Ecoepic
Part IV.

Emergence

Believe me friends
The truth is not that far beyond our reach
I've glimpsed it several times my self
Once while at the beach
Gazing at that perfect line
Where ocean meets sky
Time stood still . . . my heart slowed down
Something waited for me when I die . . .

Another time, while meditating in a chair
A radiance began to flare
Brighter than but somewhat akin
To sheet-lightning
Without rumble or rain
And much too vast to fit within
The confines of my humble brain
I thought I left my body, then
As soon as I became aware
I found myself back in my chair
The light went dim again

After that I often tried
To find that place I can't describe
Occasionally I did succeed
But always only fleetingly

So mysterious and so profound
Those supernal disconnections from the ground

Try it!
Find a comfortable place to sit
Relax your body, fingers, toes
Close your eyes and look inside
Breathe slowly through your nose
Let the waves of thought subside
Imagine not needing any clothes
Idle your senses, expand your essence
Enter that deep purple zone
Where rods and cones deprived of light
Concoct a vision of their own

A vision of Utopia as nothing more
Than a collective state of mind
Where all perceive the days in store
As better than the ones behind
Where history is widely perceived
As net progress toward a common goal
Engendered by spreading awareness
That we are part of a larger whole
Our bodies are part of Gaia's body
Our souls are part of her soul

Our brains together comprise her brain
Only by us can she know and be known
Her numinous mind an emergent property
Arising from the chaos of our own

Utopia can accommodate imperfection
The trend is all that counts
If we're moving in the right direction
All our steps will have a bounce
Perfection itself is an elusive goal
Beyond a gap we never close
Its image helps direct our work
And changes as our knowledge grows
As our *current best explanations* evolve
Are grasped, symbolized, articulated
Transformed into culture
And assimilated

Good ideas don't go away
they mature with each generation
- peace
- animal rights
- sustainability
- slavery supplanted by arbitration

Why should some work overtime
While others are unemployed
Victims of a circumstance
They didn't know how to avoid?

Let thy neighbor share thy job
There's plenty of work to distribute
Pass the burdens and benefits around
We all want and need to contribute

Eventually most of the work will be done
What's left will be a source of enjoyment
As we join together to sustain
A natural economy
That maximizes unemployment

By emphasizing maintenance
Of everything ever manufactured
From computer chips to rocket ships
Roads buildings infrastructure

Paint and varnish, polish and buff
Protect from weather rust and ruin
There's pleasure in fixing broken stuff
Or using the parts to make a new one

Loosen the screws, disassemble
Arrange the pieces all in a line
Consult the manual
so that's how it works!
Admire the clever design

And whatever items are made anew
Are crafted with pride and care
With intent to make them last forever
Easy to upgrade and repair
Making full use of recycled materials
Land fills no longer there

When we rub our hands against
Ancestral handles smooth 'n worn
We feel at once the common sense
Of saving things for those unborn
That sense of continuity
Between the generations
Reinforced by maintenance
Sustained by education

The centerpieces of our civilization
Are the neighborhood schools, solid gleaming
Ever better symbols of our appreciation
For being alive, engaged, not dreaming
For having been raised in community
And taught the truth from K thru 12
In colorful windowful classless rooms
Where older children help the young
And thereby learn about themselves

Where students learn to love to learn
By watching parents continue to study
If you no be learnin' you no be livin'
That be the motto for everybody
Where biology is taught in the local preserve
And recess is often prolonged
Where the only bells that ever ring
Are those in the blue jay's song

Nurture respect for all living things
For Nature and the *Gentle Way*
For the calloused hands of history
By which we prosper every day
If you no be learnin', You just be wastin'
Your precious life away

Show children how to grow things green
To know from whence their sustenance derives
How to make music, dance and sing
Whistle yodel harmonize
How to identify flora and fauna
Birds by their voices, songs and calls
The wood thrush plays his flute at dawn
And again when evening falls
The Whip Poor Will repeats his name
After dark, as do Chuck Will's Widows
Night Herons complain with a "quock" or a "quark"
Mockingbird verses have 3 to 5 dittos
To know wild mammals from the cast of their scat
Insects by pitch of buzz or drone
Deciduous trees by weave of bark
Conifers by shape of needle and cone
Teach them how to deduce and compute
To distinguish fiction from fact
How by reducing consumption of carbon
One can avoid a Pigovian tax
(that levied incentive that steers us down
the path of conserving a natural resource)
Ecological Economics
Like Language and Math
Is a required perennial course

Religion -
Don't burden the children with dreary dogma
Nor abuse them with unfounded threats
Of eternal suffering, fire and brimstone
Such hogwash too often psychosis begets

Let them discover religion on their own
In a green cathedral near their home
Beneath a vault of massive trees
Feet in touch with moss and leaves
Pondering Gaia's mysteries

They will return with heavy questions
Some of whose answers are unknown
Then is the time for their induction
After the spiritual seeds have been sewn
Begin a program of religious instruction
Leverage nature's magnetism
Let natural history become the scripture
Ecology the catechism.

= = = = = =

Imagine!
Streams meandering through neighborhoods
Houses kept to the higher contours
Roof-water flowing above the ground
Not below in dark storm sewers
Soaking, filtering through worm-worked soil
Replenishing the aquifers
Cool clean Aquapristine®
To quench the thirst of connoisseurs
Wild flowers in each backyard
At the edge of protected green spaces
An elaborate labyrinth of genetic exchange
And with Gaia's good graces

There will be:

Panthers interbreeding from Key West to Nome
Wolves ascending from Mexico to Maine
Diversity thriving throughout the biome
Homo neosapiens tending the links in the chain

Forests mountains deserts prairies
Their depths accessible only by foot
Entry requires a valid permit
And a promise to leave things put

Rules, rules -
Will there always be rules?
Yes, a few - but don't despair
Just keep them simple
Consistent and fair
Revise and update every December
Try to improve them over time
Make them easy to remember
By insisting that they rhyme
For example:
1)
The fruition of the human species
Must not exceed that which allows
The on site mulching of its feces
And the same for chickens pigs and cows
2)
Graduation from l'école secondaire
Requires full compliance
With practical standards of how to repair
At least one major appliance
3)
Stay in your lane, pass on the left
When pedaling where once were traffic jams
Keep your skateboard on leash when in motion
Always yield to busses and trams

4)

Earth First! People Second!

Animals are not for food or attire

No motorized recreation

No manufacturing weapons of fire

5)

No more roads in the national forests

Maintain wide buffer zones

Log only with helicopters and horses

Leave some old trees to die on their own

6)

Thou shalt not kill

Thou shalt not steal

Thou shalt not covet thy neighbor's house

Love thy neighbor as thy self

But do not have sex with thy neighbors spouse

Thou shalt not lie

Nor worship false idols

To blaspheme is most lowly

Honor thy parents as long as they live

Remember the Sabbath and keep it holy

Amen

Glory be to Gaia
Glory be to clean air, her breath
Glory be to clean water, her blood
Glory be to earth her body, fire her spirit
Glory be to all species

And now . . . .

Your meditation is almost done
Your head begins to nod
You turn your face up toward the sun
You sense somehow there is a god
With opening eyes you contemplate
The meaning of the place you've been
Determined - Yes! - to actuate
The values culled from deep within
You vow to focus all your powers
On the only goal that matters
To discover how we all can live
In peace, in love
In collective awe of
This beautiful planet of ours

Other Poems

What Good is Poetry?

Words can't explain why nothing bites
On a hot Cacapon afternoon
Or describe the shapes that water makes
Flowing over stones
The way each swirl dissipates
In time for another
How a barely submerged boulder
Makes its presence known
By pointing a wake upstream
Parting water like a miracle.

Curses not verses are what I need
When the hungry mother of large-mouth bass
That lurks beneath that over-leaning sycamore
Tastes every morsel drifting by
With the sole exception of my artificial fly.

And words alone will never keep
No matter how arranged
The pig and chicken factory waste
From seeping into even this
The cleanest river east of Colorado

dedicated to Peg Norman

Plea of the Pond

dusk is tune up time
each new April evening star
commands another member of the choir
to respond
one by one they audition
and I am positioned
where the maestro would stand
as curtains of darkness unveil
the pond

a bat meanders aimfully
against a waxing gibbus
devouring mosquitos
over the dark wet surface
from which this music pours
relentlessly
without intermission
that their transmissions
might be received
by intelligent life on this planet

several species voices weaving
in and out of synchrony
a few nearby, loud but wise
sense my aura when I rise
the decibels subside
and then resume
a dozen mantras
leave no room for thoughts in me
I become a channel for the plea
of the pond

ngelp! ngelp!
the Rana scream through me
who lingers for at least an hour
wondering how or why
we let so many ponds go dry
or sour from pollution
who sees the decline
in numbers of their kind
as cause for revolution

Connecting with Creation

While having breakfast on the porch
reading cereal box ingredients
through a magnifying glass
a high-pitched familiar hum
descends like a miniature Huey
over the great mammalian landscape of my arm.
It touches down, stumbles around
tripping over hairs
divining a perfect spot to drill.
I focus the glass with my other hand.
It lifts up, hovers, and docks at last
then slips its feeble proboscis in between
two epidermal fibroblasts.

Mosquitoes, unlike some phlebotomists
never seem to miss the vein.
A few nanoliters of anticoagulant
cause not pain but acute itching
an impulse to blow the intruder away.
But soon the itching subsides
as if withdrawn with the first blood.
The translucent belly swells up pink
to several times its empty size.

Then laboring with my heavy gift, it drifts away
 got to lay some eggs today before the frost
it crashes at the edge of the pond
where a salamander loiters by the mud
changing colors in the sun.
He snatches that mosquito with his tongue
swallows it together with my blood.

That afternoon I hear a splash
Look up to see the ripples dissipate.
Can't help but wonder
 what that fish just ate?
And later, on another day
 I bow my head and pray
Thankful for the fish upon my plate.

Dead Wood

. . . . . . and then, much later,
after hundreds of layers of cambium
had numbered her girth
the spirit withdrew. Suddenly,
with as little notice as when
it had first arrived on earth,
squeezing its huge mystery
into that tiny acorn.
Her breathing stopped.
No buds or leaves appeared.
What in winter had been just
another naked figure in the crowd
now stood out like David
bones and muscles all exposed.
Dead, of course, but still erect and proud
a monument to her own passing,
tall above the remnants
of her final and most fruitful fall.

The canopy is broken now,
Poison ivy shinnies up her trunk,
hoisted by the very light that built
the thing to which it clings.
Ants and termites follow close behind

finally free to cross the line
they hollow out the heart of her.
Instead of warblers and thrushes
come flickers and woodpeckers
daily paying their noisy respects
peeling back the skin, partaking
of her body by the insect full.
Instead of raging katydids
at night come softly spoken owls
to assess the broken sockets
of her moon-engaging hull.

One by one her limbs succumb
to weight of vine and snow.
Winds blow hard, she cannot bend
her roots let go, she tips, and then . . .
her lumbering carcass comes to rest
amongst the rocks and flowers
in the understory of her youth.
Prayerful chipmunks eulogize.
Mulching worms and micro-organisms
tenderize what's left of her.
Old molecules and rare earth ions
seek asylum in the rain,
penetrate the hairy roots,
and rise up through the xylem of her progeny

A Cappela Gold

(after Peg Millett's album Gentle Warrior)

Your music
Makes me long for wildhood
Swamps ponds lakes and woods
Tangled fence rows separating pastures
From rotating crops
And smelly summer fallow

I love walking up hill

Perhaps my mother sang like that
While she carried me
All the way to term
But never remarried
Then taught me how to harmonize
To part my hair this way
And play these riffs
While you take breaths
Between the lines
Of your *Forever Wild*

Oh lady of deep ecology

unquavering essence of Earth First!
keep on singing, keep uncompromising
in defense of Mother Earth.
Aweeya!
Aweeya!
Aweeya!

Whose Duck?

Shots could be heard for over a mile
The hunter's face relaxed in a smile
A wood duck plummeted through the sky
Bee-bees lodged by wing and eye
One hundred pounds of black labrador
Plunged into the chilly reservoir
On the opposite shore, with sun in her face
Stood a woman, watching the deadly chase
Through skillfully focused binoculars
She admired the duck, the brilliant colors
Green and purple and blue, luminescent
The thought of its dying was very unpleasant
And not far beyond swam the ebony retriever
The desire to please in its eyes like a fever

The duck was wounded but still could paddle
It reached the bank and waddled
Up the slope where the woman waited
Unlike any the hunter had dated
This one had been in a lot of fights
An ardent defender of animal rights
She had a presence there in the wood
Firm, like the ground on which she stood

The duck's painful journey finally ended
At the feet of the woman as if it depended
On her to save it from further harm
She took it decisively into her arms
Small quacks of fear emerged from its throat
So she tucked it inside her dark winter coat
Where next to her bosom it settled down
Despite the yelping of the ebony hound
Which, reaching the shore, paused for a shake
Then picked up the scent of the wounded drake
And ran towards the woman, ran right past her
Eager to finish a job for its master
Losing the scent it turned around
Facing the woman who stood her ground
And spoke to the hound "Go home!" ... "Stay!"
But the dripping wet hulk did not obey
Fixed on the scent that emerged from her breast
It slowly advanced, a growl in its chest

"Back off!" said the hunter, emerging from his truck
And then, to the woman "Have you seen my duck?"
A duck which only moments before
Was wild and free, unaccounted for
Feeling a stir beneath her coat
She turned to the hunter and cleared her throat

"I'll keep the duck" the woman said
"It maybe can't fly but its not dead.
I'll take it home 'til it gets back its nerve
Then turn it loose in a game preserve"

"That duck belongs to me" he replied
The dog was restless, still rumbling inside
The woman turned and walked toward her car
"Wait a minute! Who do you think you are?"
He followed her, took hold of her wrist
"Don't touch me!" she said, unmistakably pissed
Her hair glistened in the evening sun
Her shapely denims broke into a run
The dog chased behind, nipping, touching
She tripped over him, the duck still clutching
As she tried to get up, the dog with a heave
Knocked her down, tugged violently at her sleeve
Its teeth accidentally punctured her skin
Blood rose to the surface . . did rabies go in?

"Back off, Bituminous!" the hunter thundered
The dog was confused, unaware of its blunder
At the tone of its master's voice it came cowering
The duck's scent almost but not quite overpowering
The hunter pointed and nodded toward the pickup

A signal Bituminous had known since a pup
He leaped into the cab through a window left open
Sat there panting, tongue hanging, mouth open

The woman escaped to her car, locked the door
While wrapping the duck in her coat on the floor
She noticed the blood on her hand, felt the pain
Got some on her jeans, made a dark stain
She reached for the keys, then came a reminder
The hunter's truck was parked right behind her
She rolled down the window, unwilling to smile
"The dog's had shots but its been a while
You'd better see a doctor soon
Let me drive you to the emergency room"

They rode in the truck, not speaking, just glancing
Bituminous in the back with darkness advancing
They reached the clinic and parked the truck
He opened the door, she got out with the duck
"You're taking it with you?" he said in amazement
She started with the bundle across the pavement
"What did you expect me to do?
Leave it there in the truck with you?
You tried to fill it with lead!
If it weren't for me this duck would be dead!"

The hunter shook his head, "I've done nothing wrong"
To the dog he said "Stay" and followed along

Inside, as usual, the myriads were seated
Impatiently waiting their turn to be treated
"Your insurance card please?" she fumbled
in her purse
Then transferred the bundle to him with a curse
"I'll keep your coat while your busy, hon.
I promise to give it back when you're done"

Back in the lobby the hunter was struck
By the feel of the life of a wild duck
The warmth, the breathing, the gentle beating
Of the heart of the thing
that he would have been eating
He stroked its body and breathed a prayer
Made a small opening to provide some air
People gathered around, children and moms
"Can it fly?" said one of the littlest ones
The duck was now peaking out of the coat
"Not yet" said the hunter, a lump in his throat
"We'll take it home 'til it gets back its nerve
And then set it free in a game preserve"

Mother's Day in Rock Creek Park

Sitting alone
On a carpet of lesser celendine
In a Rock Creek flood zone
6 a.m.
Celebrating Mother's day
By being what I am
Being what she made of me
Beneath these bark-stemmed glasses
Drinking in the green that overflows
Especially from the sapling goblets
Oh! she would have said
See how this one grows!
A Cardinal's toast is echoed
By the clinking of a towhee
Kerplunk! I swear! A squirrel falls
Right next to me! Bounces up
And scampers on its way
Two wrens pursue a jay

Feeling chilly, comes the sun
Filling glasses all around
Splashing bright green bubbly on the ground

I cross my legs close my eyes
And listen to the sounds
Of downies robbins flickers and others
Whose names she taught
And I forgot so soon
While trying to remember
Where I was before the womb

Oh Mother of mine
From Mother Earth
From whom we all ascended
Where do you be?
Within your grave?
I'd misbehave if I believed
That that was where it ended

Cocktail Conversation

Ask "How's it goin" and "What ya been doing"?
Trivial questions galore
Mention the weather, tell a good joke
Listen to tales of yore
Bitch about taxes, inflation, the dollar
Pollution, abortion, welfare, and more
Lament the lack of mass transportation
But don't mention nuclear war
No - mustn't remind us of nuclear war.

Declare what you wish on religion or science
And politics - whatever you say
Incidentally, if you don't mind my asking
How much do you weigh?
With such an array of meaningful options
Why touch on a subject of horror?
Have another drink and I'll have one too
If you don't mention nuclear war
Not yet - not nuclear war.

Elaborate on children, your neighbor's, your own
Decry the condition of the schools
What do you think they'll do when they're grown
If the future is left to the fools?

Take pride in their latest athletic achievements
Be sure to remember the score
And when you've exhausted your final excuse
Only then mention nuclear war -
Say it softly - Nuclear War.

Don't give the impression of over concern
Be thoughtful, sincere, don't get sore
Nor hang your head in helpless defeat
Breathe deep, and finish the chore
Remember your aim and stay on the mark
Suppress that terrifying roar
The only issue demanding attention
Is the threat of nuclear war -
Eliminate Nuclear War!

O wls nesting

L ogs not taken for a hundred years; no stumps

D ead wood standing
   or leaning on neighbors

G aps in the canopy
   large sun flecks nurture saplings

R egeneration happens (slowly)

O rganic activity abounds
   fungi microbes ants worms

W oodpeckers till the cellulose
   husband termites

T opology of pits and mounds
   trees long ago uprooted

H ollowed trees, home to fury animals
   hallowed haven to hikers

Freedom

Freedom is a rich and powerful word
Connoting a lack of constraint, a feel
Of being in charge, out from under
As when driving my first automobile
Oh what I'd give for one clear photo
Of myself behind the wheel
Of that 1954 Customline Ford
And close by my side, that beautiful girl

I've had liberty all my life
Some would say I don't deserve it
Having protested against wars
That they said were fought to preserve it
Now another country has been invaded
In the name of freedom (in retrospect)
While freedom at home is vitiated
By "signing statements" and the Patriot Act

Oh purple mountains, travesties
Clear cut, pushed over, tops removed
Freedom of enterprise and LLC's
Of this I disapprove:
This filling in of creeks and streams

This ravaging of the land
This manifestation of lack of esteem
For the perfect work of a slow steady hand

Don't lecture me about fighting for freedom
It's a concept I have long understood
While fighting construction of another beltway
Mansionization of my neighborhood
While working on the grass roots campaign
Of a candidate of my persuasion
This is freedom. This is my right.
This is my obligation.

I am endangered

And dangerously so
I could go berserk tomorrow
Cause damage, hurt somebody
Call it a nervous breakdown

I am a subspecies in decline
My favorite habitat dwindles
Each generation brings fewer of my kind
And more of the others

They call me names
They call me pagan tree hugger
It doesn't hurt
Calling me what I'm proud to be

They don't know
That if I go
They will follow
I am a canary

God Was

To tell the truth I know
that I've been lied to heretofore,
I know that I've been fooled
and led astray
I used to think that men
were not to blame for what's in store,
That Science or the Lord
would find a Way
Yes, chemistry, math and medicine
would save the world, God willin'
Then they said that God was dead,
that Science was the villain
I should have been more sensitive
to inward inclination,
Instead of searching outwardly
for hope and inspiration
'Cause deep inside my mind I know
there hides a glimpse of what could be
A purple glow, a flash, a flow
the hints of immortality

Light Answers to Heavy Questions
(asked by adolescents back from the woods)

1. Who am I?

You my child are
The product of a passionate joining
On a wild night after a dance
Your parents decided to take a chance
One of Daddy's spermatozoa
Collided with one of Mummy's ova
In the back seat of a second hand Chevy Nova
The two became a zygote deep inside her
Then over and over that zygote divided
Your pregnant mummy soon had a patch
Of cells attached to her uterine wall
That blastocyst ontogenized, continued to sprout
Became a thriving embryo
With eyes and snout
A neural tube, a beating heart
And limbs that began to twitch
In a way that startled Daddy
When he rubbed oil on those faint marks
Where Mummy's tummy had begun to stretch

Somewhere betwixt conception and birth
At a point in time even you can't recall
(exactly when is fiercely debated
though nobody has a clue)
Your soul arrived from outer space
To occupy a special place
In the new community of cells
        that became you.

Were you hungry? Oh my Gaia!
You latched onto your Mummy's breast
With a ferocity that made her wince
And when you first smiled we were convinced
That miracles are more than ideas

2. Why am I here?

Perhaps not
Because you're supposed to be
But rather because you chose
To squeeze your unbounded essence
Down into that tiny fetal orbit
(The way a wave of blue light
Is absorbed by the color of unborn flesh)

Your spirit could have started fresh
In another galaxy, on another planet
(did you encounter any as nice as this?)
Or, still here,
but in a newly hatched northern gannet
Or maybe some other threatened species
(if one had been ready when you were)
Or trapped in the ridiculously minuscule
seed of a giant sequoia
(waiting for lightning to strike the fire)

Yes, you could have searched further
For the ideal host, but . . .
(now facing the child, squeeze the shoulders,
cup the back of the neck in your hands)
. . . this, my love, is what you selected
This coalition of a gazillion cells
       that stand for you
       the One elected
       to envision and direct
       what they become
So exercise and feed them well
Breath deeply through your nose
Bend like a sapling in every direction
Strive to perfect a yoga pose

Stand like a heron at the water's edge
Sit cross-legged with hands in lap
Use your brain to dig and dredge
For evidence to fill the gaps
In the creation story of how our kind
Unique, so far as we know, in our mind
Evolved as a twig - or is it a leaf
At the end of a long and deciduous branch
The only species able to conceive
This metaphor - and blanch.

3. What happens when we die?

To the question of life after death
Answer yes! Why not let optimism prevail?
I hope so. I think so. I wish. I guess.
And if they press for more detail
Be honest, admit you just don't know
But also be quick to submit
That absence of proof
Doesn't obviate truth
Doesn't mean anything couldn't be so

After all
There must be something
To this weird mystery
The way we sit here face to face
Each of us a talking galaxy
Of fundamental particles, a mist
A cloud of charge, of mostly empty space
Yet somehow disposed
   to love and embrace
      to laugh and gesticulate
Like swarms of gnats
We hover close and speculate
On what might happen when
Our swarms disintegrate

I remember spending a bright afternoon
Alone on my back in the middle of a meadow
Binoculars focused on a white quarter moon
When into my view came a lone black buteo
Riding up air currents in near perfect circles
With barely a flick of a feather
Gradually vanishing deep in the sky
Leaving me, still prone, to wonder whether
That's what happens when we die

Massless, ethereal, no longer embodied
No longer stuck in a cluster of dust
No longer subject to gravity (or friction)
Like spider silk in a summer gust
We rise beyond the celestial sphere
All ties to the earth forsaking
All memories of our short life here
Fade like dreams after waking

Careening through the universe
(avoiding black holes)
We search for heaven sublime
Or maybe a new hospitable planet
With exotic life forms for our souls to inhabit
For another brief moment in time

Acknowledgments

To Manley for feeding my environmental angst
To Tom for unfailing affirmation
To Ljubiša for reliable hugs, pats on the back
and the occasional kiss
To Leonid & Co. for salvaging my day job
To Frank & Donna for being like family
To John, Thea, Norbert, Elaine, Father McNarley
and Sister Hallie for friendship of the warmest kind
To Phil for inexhaustible exuberance
To Adrienne for the little brown journal
To Kent for turning me on to nature literature
To Lisa and Geraldine for boosting my confidence
To Ali and Kris for thriving on my love
To Jack & Hawk for memorizing parts of this book
To, finally and most of all, Glenda for tolerating,
indeed nursing, my obsession

Five of the "other poems" appeared previously:
Whose Duck, Dead Wood, Mother's Day and
Plea of the Pond in *The Audubon Naturalist*
and What Good is Poetry in *Potomac Review*.

About the Pictures

Cover - Aspen forest with wild flowers near Ohio Pass in southwestern Colorado.

p. 6 - Saguaro Cacti in the Superstition Wilderness, east of Phoenix Arizona.

p.11 - Ribbon diagram depicting the backbone folding of part of a protein, the fibronectin type III domain.

p. 24 - Skyscape in Toronto, Ontario.

p.35 - Boys will be boys. These three like to ride their toys in Crabtree State Forest, one of the few remaining patches of old growth in Maryland.

p.36 - Osprey and fish in loblolly pine at Blackwater Wildlife Refuge. Photo by Elaine Kampmueller.

p. 74 - Birch and Sycamore trees near the C&O Canal, Potomac River Watershed.

p.88 - The author's traibin (half trailer, half cabin) at Briary Bottom, West Virginia, where many of the words herein were written.

p.107- The author (left) with Garrett Park Citizens Association President Gene McDowell and Mayor Peggy Pratt in 1982, when our town became a Nuclear Free Zone, first in the USA.

p.120 - A few of the hundreds of wind turbines near Palm Springs, California.

About the Author

Ken Ingham was born in Ann Arbor, Michigan on Valentines day, 1942. A second-generation urbanite, he grew up in the suburbs of Detroit while spending boyhood summers with Aunt Helen and Uncle Gordon on a farm near Shelbyville. He majored in chemistry and mathematics at Eastern Michigan Univ and earned a PhD in physical

chemistry at the Univ of Colorado. He spent 29 years researching blood proteins for the American Red Cross, while raising, with his wife Glenda, two daughters, Alison Blakely and Kristen Mullaney. He resides in the town of Garrett Park, MD 20896-0258.

Additional samples of the author's writing
may be seen at www.nethingham.org